ALSO BY PHILIP LEVINE

POETRY

News of the World (2009)
Breath (2004)
The Mercy (1999)
Unselected Poems (1997)
The Simple Truth (1994)
What Work Is (1991)
New Selected Poems (1991)
A Walk with Tom Jefferson (1988)
Sweet Will (1985)
Selected Poems (1984)
One for the Rose (1981)
7 Years from Somewhere (1979)
Ashes: Poems New and Old (1979)
The Names of the Lost (1976)
1933 (1974)
They Feed They Lion (1972)
Red Dust (1971)
Pili's Wall (1971)
Not This Pig (1968)
On the Edge (1963)

ESSAYS

My Lost Poets (2016)
So Ask (2003)
The Bread of Time (1994)

TRANSLATIONS

Off the Map: Selected Poems of Gloria Fuertes (1984)
Edited and translated with Ada Long
Tarumba: The Selected Poems of Jaime Sabines (1979)
Edited and translated with Ernesto Trejo

INTERVIEWS

Don't Ask (1981)

THE LAST SHIFT

THE LAST SHIFT

POEMS BY

PHILIP LEVINE

EDITED BY EDWARD HIRSCH

Alfred A. Knopf · NEW YORK · 2016

This Is a Borzoi Book
Published by Alfred A. Knopf

Copyright © 2016 by The Estate of Philip Levine

All rights reserved. Published in the United States by Alfred A. Knopf, a division of
Penguin Random House LLC, New York, and distributed in Canada by Random House of
Canada Limited, Toronto.

www.aaknopf.com/poetry

Knopf, Borzoi Books, and the colophon are registered trademarks of Penguin Random House LLC.

Library of Congress Cataloging-in-Publication Data
Names: Levine, Philip, 1928–2015
Title: The last shift : poems / Philip Levine.
Description: First edition. | New York : Alfred A. Knopf, 2016. | "This is a Borzoi book."
Identifiers: LCCN 2016012060 (print) | LCCN 2016018517 (ebook) |
ISBN 9780451493262 (hardcover) | ISBN 9780451493286 (ebook)
Subjects: | BISAC: POETRY / American / General.
Classification: LCC PS3562.E9 A6 2016 (print) | LCC PS3562.E9 (ebook) |
DDC 811/.54—dc23
LC record available at https://lccn.loc.gov/2016012060

Jacket photograph by EyeEm Mobile GmbH/Alamy
Jacket design by Chip Kidd

Manufactured in the United States of America
First Edition

CONTENTS

III

FOREWORD

Philip Levine selected the poems for this volume, but he left it to me, as his friend and literary executor, to organize and title it. This is the final book of his own making, and I've tried to honor his achievement. This title has the elegiac shadings of a last book, but I hope it also celebrates all that he brought into American poetry. He was a poet of the night shift, a late, ironic Whitman of our industrial heartland, and his life's work is a long assault on isolation, an ongoing struggle against the enclosures of suffering. Looking back, I would say that his poetry began in rage, ripened toward elegy, and culminated in celebration. All three moods—anger, grief, and, finally, joy—are present in this collection, his last book on the job.

Philip Levine created a fundamentally human-centered poetry. He writes here of his childhood, adolescence, and early manhood in Detroit, which takes on an almost legendary quality now that everything is gone—the factories, the machines, the night workers. Time itself becomes the subject, the mystery. Here is one of his working-class aubades:

> *8 a.m. and we punch out*
> *and leave the place to our betters,*
> *the day-shift jokers who think*
> *they're in for fun. It's still Monday*
> *2,000 miles and fifty years*
> *later and at my back I always*

hear Chevy Gear & Axle
grinding the night-shift workers
into antiquity.

Levine writes of his travels, especially to out-of-the-way European places, where he often finds what is funny, overlooked, and neglected, though he keeps returning to his primary cities: Detroit, Fresno, Brooklyn. He combines lyrical and narrative values, and his pointed anecdotes amplify into a larger vision. He is a poet of social justice and memory, a singer who enjoined himself to stand up for the victimized and the disenfranchised. The rages of his early work still burn ("Oh / to be young and strong and dumb / again in Michigan!"), but they no longer threaten to thwart or silence him. There is a comic tone to some of these remembrances, a mournful quality to many others, but there is also something else. He was a poet who refused to quit. "Let's just give it what we have / and when that's done give it a second time," he declares in "More Than You Gave." I would say that the Generation of '27 (Federico García Lorca, Miguel Hernández, Rafael Alberti) and other martyred leaders of the Spanish Civil War (such as Francicso Ferrer Guardia, Buenaventura Durruti, and Francisco Ascaso) gave him a utopian politics, a blueprint for the future, a visionary hope that continued to sustain him. Thus his poems recall the fallen, but they also take up the anarchist dream of freedom and justice, the chant "We shall inherit." Here, as elsewhere in his work, he memorializes a lost world and envisions a new one.

In editing this book, I have tried to keep in mind two of Phil's deepest values: his fervent belief in poetry and his ferocious loyalty to the past. He often praised, in life and work, the stubborn will of the dispossessed to dig in and endure. That determination is at the heart of his central project. The motif of regeneration and rebirth resounds throughout his work, which, for all of its denunciations, ends as poetry of praise for "a world / that runs one and one at its own sweet will." He was ultimately a Romantic poet, an American Keats, who believed in the boundlessness of human possibility. We are lucky to have had him among us.

Edward Hirsch

I

INHERITANCE

A rectangular Bulova, my Zayde
called a dress watch, I wore it for years,
and though it gave the wrong time
I treasured the sense of community
it offered, the beauty of certain numerals —
the seven especially, the way it leaned
into its subtle work and never changed,
and signified exactly what it was
and no more. In dreams I learned
that only the watch and the circle
of ash trees surrounding me, and the grass
prodding my bare feet, and of course
my nakedness, were necessary, though
common. Just surrendering my youth,
I still believed everything in dreams
meant something I could parse to discover
who we were.
As I write these words
in sepia across a lined page, I have
no idea why they've taken the shape
I've given them, some cursive, some not,
some elegantly articulated, others plain,
many of no use at all. They go on working
as best they can, like the Parker 51
that spent its coming of age stumbling
backwards into Yiddish or the Bulova
that finally threw up its twin baroque arms
in surrender to the infinite and quit
without a word. The Parker still works
and is never to blame. On good days
it works better than I, and when it leaks
it leaks only ink, never a word best
left unsaid.
As a boy I would steal

into Zayde's bedroom, find the watch
in a velvet box, wind it, hold it
to each ear—back then both worked—
to hear its music, the jeweled wheels
and axles that kept time alive.
There is still such joy in these tokens
from back of beyond: the watch,
the Parker pen, the tiny pocketknife
he used to separate truth from lies,
the ivory cigarette holder—
a gift, he claimed, from FDR
who mistook him for a famous
Russian violinist. I could call them
"Infinite riches in a little room"
or go cosmic and regard them
as fragments of a great mystery
instead of what they are,
amulets against nothing.

MY BROTHER, THE ARTIST, AT SEVEN

As a boy he played alone in the fields
behind our block, six frame houses
holding six immigrant families,
the parents speaking only gibberish
to their neighbors. Without the kids
they couldn't say "Good morning" and be
understood. Little wonder
he learned early to speak to himself,
to tell no one what truly mattered.
How much can matter to a kid
of seven? Everything. The whole world
can be his. Just after dawn he sneaks
out to hide in the wild, bleached grasses
of August and pretends he's grown up,
someone complete in himself without
the need for anyone, a warrior
from the ancient places our fathers
fled years before, those magic places:
Kiev, Odessa, the Crimea,
Port Said, Alexandria, Lisbon,
the Canaries, Caracas, Galveston.
In the damp grass he recites the names
over and over in a hushed voice
while the sun climbs into the locust tree
to waken the houses. The husbands leave
for work, the women return to bed, the kids
bend to porridge and milk. He advances
slowly, eyes fixed, an animal or a god,
while beneath him the earth holds its breath.

YOUR TURN

A ruined Chevy, the windshield
gone, the seats dragged out
into the weeds, the guts trailing

off into the orchard, if seven trees
make an orchard. On the porch looms
the proud white refrigerator

never paid for. Where are the kids,
all blond, all dirty, all barefoot?
Hiding in the weeds? These kids

are too full of juice to hide that long.
They could be crawling under
the house where the dirt reeks

of fish bait or in the silo playing
kiss your uncle or upstairs
lounging in papa's golf clothes

like real people. You won't
find them in the blurred photos
of class reunions, you won't

see them posed on the calendar
that hangs behind the barber
as he whisks talcum on your neck,

snaps the sheet clean of curls,
and cries out in a voice heard
only in hell, "Who's next?"

1934

You might hear that after dark in towns
like Detroit packs of wild dogs took over
the streets. I was there. It never happened.
In the old country before the Great War,
my people were merchants and butchers,
and then the killings drove the family
first to England, then Canada, then here.
My father's brother had a shoe repair shop
for a time on Brush Street; he'd learned
the trade from his father back in Kiev.
My mother's family was in junk. The men
were huge, thick-chested, with long arms
and great scarred hands. My uncle Leo
could embrace a barrel of scrap metal,
laugh out his huge laugh, and lift it up
just for the joy. His wife, Rebecca,
let her hair grow out in great wiry tangles
and carried her little fists like hammers.
Late summer Sundays we'd drive out
to the country and pick armloads
of sweet corn, boil them in sugar,
and eat and eat until we couldn't.
Can you believe those people would let
dogs take what was theirs, would cross
an ocean and a continent to let
anyone or anything dictate?
After dark these same men would drink
out on the front steps. The neighbors claimed
they howled at the moon. Another lie.
Sometimes they told stories of life
back in Russia, stories I half-believed
of magic escapes and revenge killings,
of the gorgeous Ukrainian girls they had.
One night they tore up the lawn wrestling until

Leo triumphed, Leo in his vested suit,
gray and sweat stained. My uncle Josef
was different; tall and slender, he'd
come into the family through marriage
here in Michigan. A pensive, gentle man,
when stray dogs came to the back door
of the shoe shop he'd let them in, even
feed them. Their owners, he told me,
barely had enough to feed themselves.
Uncle Josef would take a battered pair
of work shoes and cut the soles off
with a hooked cobbler's knife and then
drawing one nail at a time from his mouth,
pound on a new sole. He'd pry off
the heel and do the same. I was just a kid,
seven at most, and never tired of watching
how at the polishing wheel the leather
took on its color and began to glow.
Once he made a knife for me, complete
with a little scabbard that looped
around my belt. The black handle too
was leather, taken from a boot no one
reclaimed. He pounded and shaped it
until it felt like stone. Whenever you're
scared, he told me, just rub the handle
three times and nothing bad can happen.

LEAVES

The Chevy stamping plant
commandeered by clans
of enormous rats so skilled
in their pursuit of life
they devoured intricate
machine parts believed
inedible. Five nights
a week you lived there—
this was in '46—; and when
a long-awaited spring
arrived nothing changed.
From heaven you could have
looked down on rows
of parked Chevys dozing
toward afternoon, you could
have imagined trees
growing in their stead,
elms—thousands of them—
their sticky leaves budding
out as they once did outside
the bedroom window.
You could have conjured
a pale climbing rose that
gathered dust, glass,
automobile exhaust,
the stains of melted snow,
to transform into blood-
tipped thorns, for thorns
too need to live. Not far off,
you told yourself, you could
hear the music of eternity.
More likely it was your own
breathing, new to the job,
or if not then the constant

rise and descent of the presses,
steadier than the beating
of your heart. The presses,
too, had their assignments,
to reform scraps of old toys,
abandoned stoves, yellow
school buses, armies of picks
and shovels, their handles
stained with our fathers' lives.
That world stamped into
separate but equal steel
leaves we called springs,
springs for the generations
of Chevy cars and trucks not
yet dreamed of. The factory
is gone, the machines with it,
the night workers, you, me,
even the rats. All that's left
are these few unread words
without rhythm or breath
fading before your eyes.

THE ABSENT GARDENER

Go back to early April of 1949. Get off the Woodward streetcar
at Grand Circus Park, walk a few blocks west, and find behind
the Greyhound bus terminal a tiny garden no larger than a Buick
Roadmaster. Last week's snow is gone. It's just another morning in
Michigan, the streets dark with last night's rain, the air cool and
fresh, the pale sky so distant you wonder if this is a different world
& not last night's when the silence, windless and heavy, smelled
of rusted iron. Now the perfumes of wet black dirt, the tiny plots
marked with sticks, twine, and pebbles to hold down the warped
seed packets proclaiming their riches: radish, Big Boy tomato, Ripe
Red Wonder, little Sweetie, rhubarb, rose campion.

HISTORY

In an old photograph, you can find me picketing outside Breslin's
Plumbing & Plating. Spring, April 12, 1951, lilacs are in bloom on the
divider strip of the Outer Drive. After dark I'll cut a small branch to
give my mother. She loves both the color and the bouquet. She still
lives in the only house she ever owned. The house, the lilac bushes,
the perfume of the blooms, her joy and sadness as she places them in
a cut-glass vase my father gave her the year before he died, none of
this is in the photograph taken from the *Detroit Free Press* and pasted
in her lost scrapbook. That photograph is part of history. It's filed
on microfilm in the archives of Labor & Urban Affairs at Wayne
State and even now must be turning into dust, giving up its facts &
its faces.

ASSEMBLY

The various holy parts
of the body are presented
on a blue conveyor belt
without end. All this before
assembly. The lungs,
the liver, the kidneys
(surprisingly shaped like
beans), the roof of the mouth,
the nape, followed
by the neck, the elbows
without arms, the sac without
the testicles. One could
go on naming and naming
into the darkness hiding
in the heart, but you get
the point or if you don't
you will in time. Remember
at eighteen, brother, at Cadillac
Transmission how no one
knew what we were drilling
holes into or why except
of course for $2.85
an hour. That was after
the war when money answered
everything, and the life was
innocent or so we said
years later . . . The eyeballs,
the twin shins, the splints
for the shins, the nails
for the toes, the toes
for their nails, the stamen
for the rose, the thorns,
the buds curled so tightly
they can see absolutely nothing.

TALL TALES

Bubbie, my grandmother, proud of her English, would often on winter evenings read to me from *Oliver Twist,* usually those passages in which the boys were physically abused. She loved that book & marveled at the cunning of its elderly hero. When at four I learned to read she felt belittled & rarely spoke to me during the ensuing forty-one years. My grandfather, a tiny dapper man who loathed Bubbie, could read only Yiddish but rarely did. In order to entertain me he invented his own sagas the hero of which was also Jewish, a gigantic Siberian husky named Tommy Doggy. Tommy was amazingly resourceful &, unlike Bubbie, totally incorruptible. Whenever the Cossacks approached his village he would employ his wiles to misdirect them or frighten their horses. If need be he would take them on in hand-to-paw combat & though cruelly outnumbered he always won. One late-July evening of my seventh summer while sitting out under the stars, I asked Zayde how he knew Tommy was Jewish. We were at Walled Lake escaping the bruising heat of the city. With a snifter of Hennessey beside him, Zayde explained: like a good Jew, Tommy wrapped *tfilim* every morning, like every Jewish male he was circumcised, &—the clincher—on Shabbos he would bark only in Hebrew.

PENNSYLVANIA PASTORAL

The car stops, not because
the driver decided they'd gone
far enough or because the woman
said, "I'm sick," or the boy
had to pee. It simply stopped
because it had to, and when the
three get out and he pops
the hood they discover the fan
belt has vanished and the engine
shut down, wisely. It could
be worse, it could always be
worse—a cylinder could seize
for no foreseeable reason and send
them into irreversible debt.
Cars are, after all, only
machines, and this one—
a '48 Pontiac Six—is
aged and whimsical. It could
be much worse—the Mojave
in mid-July with no shade
in sight or northern Ontario
in winter, the snow already burning
the backs of Father's hands and
freighting Mother's lashes. They've
stalled descending into a gully
in rural Pennsylvania, a quiet
place of maples leafing out,
a place with its own creek
high in its banks and beyond
the creek a filling station,
its lights still on after dawn,
the red and green pumps ready to
give, and someone there, half-awake.

OFFICE HOURS

Midnight on Grand River, and the car barns
are quiet, the last truck left hours ago.
The watchman dreams through his rounds.

If you entered the office now you'd find
all the old upright Smith Coronas sheathed
in their gowns, the pencils tucked in drawers,

the fountain pens dreaming of the epics
they'll never write, the paper clips
holding together reports on nothing at all.

You're at the heart of a nation that divides,
adds, subtracts, and never multiplies.
Before it rings, pick up the phone,

        say in a voice you've never used before,
your Uncle Sam voice, "Yes, this is he,
tell me what you'd like to hear . . . "

and wait until the line goes dead.
Years ago you inherited all these desks
and the women who man them

        along with all the meaningless facts
that detail the profit and loss of each day.
What's it worth? You'll get your answer

from the mice as they make their way
in search of anything usable left behind.
If not from the mice, then from something else
with greater purpose and a smaller mind.

MORE THAN YOU GAVE

We have the town we call home wakening for dawn
which isn't yet here but is promised, we have

our tired neighbors rising in ones and twos, we have
the sky slowly separating itself from the houses

to become the sky while the stars blink a last time
and vanish to make way for us to enter the great stage

of an ordinary Tuesday in ordinary time. We have
our curses, our gripes, our lies all on the stale breath

of 6:37 a.m. in the city no one dreams, the Tuesday city
in which we shall live for this day or not at all.

"Where are the angels?" I ask. This is a visionary moment
in the history of time, incomplete without angels,

without at least Argente of the tarnished wings,
or the mangled half-assed Incondante who speaks

only in riddles, or one-winged Sylvania who glows
in the dark. All off in eternity doing their sacred numbers.

Instead at 6:43 a.m. we have Vartan Baghosian with a face
seamed like a softball and Minky Schantz who pitched

three games for the Toledo Mud Hens in '39 and lost
them all, we have the Volpe sisters who married

the attic on Brush Street and won't come down,
we have me, fresh as last week, bitching about my back,

my bad ankle, we have psoriasis, heartburn, the four-day
hangover, prostatitis, Jewish mothers, Catholic guilt,

we have the teenage Woodward Ave. whores going
to bed alone at last, hugging no one for that long moment

before the young madonnas rise from separate beds
to open their shutters on whatever the day presents,

to pledge their virtue and their twitching, incomparable bodies
to Jesus Christ of the Latter Day Tupperware. All this

in rooms where even in the gray dishwater dawn
the chrome grill on an Admiral black-and-white TV

gleams like the chalice of Abraham. And from his corner
the genius of this time and place, Uncle Nate, chomping

his first White Owl of the day, calls out for a doughnut
and sweetened milky coffee to dunk it in and laces up

his high-tops and swears by the vision of his blind right eye
he will have strange young pussy before the sun sets

on his miserable balding dome. Today we shall paint,
for Nate is a true artist trained in the eight-hour day

to master the necessary and not the strung-out martyrs
of El Greco or the brooding landscapes of an awful century.

No, today we paint the walls, the lintels, the ceilings,
the dadoes, and the doodads of Mrs. Victoria Settle,

formerly of Lake Park, Illinois, now come to grace
our city with the myth of her late husband, her terriers,

her fake accent, her Victorian brooches, her perfect posture,
and especially her money. Ask the gray windows

that look out on the remnants of winter a grand question:
"Have I come all the way through the fires of hell,

the torture of the dark night of the etc., so that I might inhale
the leaden fumes of Glidden Golden Gate as the dogsbody

of Nathaniel Hawthorne Glenner, the autodidact of Twelfth Street?"
It could be worse. It could be life without mortadella sandwiches,

twenty-five-cent pineapple pies, and quarts of Pilsner
at noon out on a manicured lawn in Grosse Pointe

under a sun that never before caressed an Armenian or a Jew.
We could be flogging Fuller brushes down the deadbeat streets

of Paradise Valley or delivering trunks to the dormitories
of the Episcopal ladies where no one tips or offers

a pastry and a schnapps for the longed-for trip
back to Sicily or Salonika; it could be the forge room

at Ford Rouge where the young get old fast or die trying.
So savor the hours as Nate recounts the day he hitchhiked

to Toledo only to arrive too late to see the young Dempsey
flatten Willard and claim the lily-white championship

of the world. "Story of my life," says Nate, "the last to arrive,
the first to leave." Not even Aesop could outdo our Nate,

our fabulist, whose name even is pure invention,
a confabulation of his prison reading and his twelve-year

formal education in the hobo camps of his long boyhood.
Wanderlust, he tells us, hit him at age fifteen and not

a moment too soon, for Mr. Wilson was taking boys
off to die in Europe and that was just about the time

women discovered Nate or Nate discovered women,
and they were something he wouldn't care to go without.

Call it a long day if you want and a hard one, too,
but remember we got more than we gave: we got myth,

we got music, we got underpaid work, a cheap lunch
with more to follow. On the long walk to the bus stop

and the ride home we hear the birds gathering
in the elms and maples thickening with summer finery,

and no one cares if we sing to the orange sun
that also seeks its rest, no one cares that our voices

are harsh from cigarettes and our ears worthless,
our timing off, and we've got the wrong words

in the wrong places. Let's just give it what we have
and when that's done give it a second time, one

for us and one for Nate, and even a third wouldn't hurt.

THE FUTURE

The past is no more past
than the future, or so said
Moradian, the unlikely seer
of my senior shop class.

I'll call him John, although
he was never a John or
even a Juan or a Jack,
although his surname—

Moradian—ended with "i-a-n,"
which is Ian in Scotland,
the Celtic version of John.
Our John, John Moradian,

gone sixty-seven years ago
from our schoolboy class
into the wider world of war
where his one-way ticket

got punched just the once.
I would start this again
if I could, start quietly
with a Dougie or an Alan,

both of whom made it into
their thirties, though neither
ever spoke of the past being
anything but over with.

What they actually thought
I'll never know. One spring day
the whole class went by bus
to the foundry at Ford Rouge

to see earth melted and poured
like syrup into fire. "Look up,"
someone said, maybe Dougie
or Alan, so I did and saw

way up above the collisions
of metal and men, a family
of sparrows in the trapped light,
trapped themselves, or perhaps

out to reclaim their stolen space.
Speaking of perhaps, perhaps
I'm dawdling because I haven't
seen John or Alan or Dougie

in over fifty years. Perhaps
I just like repeating their names
as though that could help them
or perhaps help me, and it does,

it helps me. They're beyond
my help. Later the class
picnicked on egg-salad
beside a wide stream that fed

our filthy river. Alan,
or maybe it was Dougie,
managed to cross the water
leaping from rock to rock

and then back again,
his balance was that good.
Alan, or maybe Dougie,
whoever had crossed, dared me

to cross, but I knew enough
not to try. I remember

the sky darkening in the east,
the bus arriving with the rain,

the windows steaming up
to hide the flooded streets.
I remember I sat next to Alan
who lied a blue streak

about an older girl who owned
her own car. The bus driver
lost the way and had to stop
at a filling station in Delray

to get directions, so the trip
was endless. I got back before
nightfall, but the day kept going
on and on into the present.

II

IMMORTAL BIRDS

There's a battered scrub jay lives
in the lemon tree in my back yard,
has a voice like tin snips dragged
across a steel file. He must think
he's a choral director; the mockers
join in to become an oratorio
of teamsters punching out.

I thought when I left Detroit
to head west I would find groves
of orange trees, a vast land tilting
slowly toward the severe peaks
of the Sierra Nevada, I thought
I'd left the corrugated world
behind in Flint and Wyandotte.

Where are the fabled birds we
read about? Miguel Hernández
climbed a tree in the Atocha park
so that Neruda might hear the song
of the nightingale. My jay jabs
his thick beak into a lemon, gargles,
and croaks out the anthems of Ecorse.

I WAS MARRIED ON THE FIFTIETH
BIRTHDAY OF PABLO NERUDA

Neither of us knew how crucial a day
it would become in the history
of poetry. He was in a Paris
bistro sipping a chilled Moulin-à-Vent
with his mistress, waiting for the chef
—a Catalan he'd favored since '39—
to deliver on the promised *mongetes amb*
botifarra he'd yearned for all that lean day,

while I was in a courthouse in Boone,
North Carolina, staring at a poster
of three auto wrecks and the one word,
"Think!" in blazing red. The circuit judge
who'd just asked me, "Do you plight your troth?"
—seeing my befuddlement—saved the day:
"Just say yes, young fellow, and we can all
move on to what you been waiting for."

SOUTH

In the cold, clear winter air
of Andalusia, I walked
a trail up through pig grass
toward a distant abandoned
farmhouse. No one could live here,
I said aloud, the land is baked clay,
the long summers are withering.
Yet someone did. The one wall
left intact bore the handprint
of a child, the fingers splayed
out to form half a message
in the lost language of childhood.
It said, "You won't find me!"
Then the wind woke from its nesting
in the weeds and the tall grass
to blow the childish words away.
Almost noon, the distant sun
rode straight above us like a God
aware of everything and like
a God utterly silent. What
could ever grow from this ground
to feed anyone? And who bore
the mysterious child who spoke
in riddles? If we climbed
the hill's crest we'd find
a higher hill and then another
hill until we reached an ocean
or gave up and turned back
to where the land descends step
by slow step to bring us exactly
here, where we began, stunned
by raw sunlight yet in the dark.

THE PRIVILEGE OF POWER

With his black-booted toe the cop awakened me. Why was I sleeping on the lawn? It was better, I told him, than the iron benches. Midafternoon in the little park near the entrance to the stadium, the sun just falling below the plane trees. By the time I got to my feet I was half awake. "Why aren't you home?" he said. "In Spain we sleep in beds." I explained I was waiting for my car to be repaired. He seemed doubtful. I must walk him to the garage & show him the car. On the way there I asked if I'd broken the law. "The law," he said. "Why do you think this has anything to do with laws?" The cafés along the Diagonal were emptying after the lunch rush. The tiny Andalusian waiter at Habana dropped his eyes & shook his head. When we entered the garage, Jordi—the boss—approached carefully. He too avoided my eyes. "May I be of service," he said. The cop told him the Dutchman claimed he had a car here. Yes, Jordi said, the white VW is his, the one on the lift. Was he sure the car belonged to the Dutchman. Yes, he brings it here many times, explained Jordi, but he is not a Dutchman, the *extranjero* is from America. *"Los Estados Unidos?"* shouted the cop, visibly shaken. He turned to me, removed his gray officer cap, half-bowed, & expressed his sorrow.

A WALL IN NAPLES AND NOTHING MORE

There *is* more, there's the perfect
blue of sky, there's a window, and hanging
from the sill what could be garments
of green cloth. Or perhaps they're rugs?
Where is everyone? you ask. Someone
must live in this house, for this wall
surely belongs to a house, why else
would there be washing on a day
of such perfect sky? You assume
that everyone is free to take in
the beach, to leisurely stroll the strand,
weather permitting, to leave shoes
and socks on a towel even here
in a city famous for petty crime.
For Thomas Jones, not the singer
the ladies threw knickers and room keys
at, but the Welsh painter, it was light
unblurring a surface until the light
became the object itself the way
these words or any others can't.
I'm doing my feeble best to entrance you
without a broad palette of the colors
which can make a thing like nothing
else, make it come alive with the grubby
texture all actual things possess
after the wind and weather batter them
the way all my years battered
my tongue and teeth until whatever
I say comes out sounding inaccurate,
wrong, ugly. Yes, ugly, the way a wall
becomes after whoever was meant
to be kept out or kept in has been
transformed perfectly into the light
and dust that collect constantly
on each object in a living world.

SICILIAN VOICES

Something very like a person
in blue work shirt and faded corduroys

lies among the pepper plants behind
the garbage dump, his face closed

to all but the ants. Climb the hill
that leads to the graveyard, open

the wooden gate, and walk slowly
among the stones, the names and dates

erased by rain. Not far off the sea
rides soundlessly toward shore;

the deaf hear it as prayer,
to the blind it is the music of eternity.

To you standing above it all
the sea is a vast panel of shades

of black and white, and the woman
off in the distance hurrying

to the scene is no one you know.
Perhaps she's the mother, perhaps not.

You should know that some day
not far off—it could be anywhere—

when the wind's voice stills,
you and the old woman will hear

the same message whispered over
and over for the rest of your lives.

You can try to answer, but you need
words for that, and you don't have any.

ANATOLE

Among all the Titans, Anatole
with his great rocky brow, his grace,
his character, was the most human.
I learned this from a local seer
who held my hands as he spoke
of Anatole's rare nature—a God
who cared for living things—
and how as an aging myth, he'd
gone off into the northern wastes
on foot to die, and found
a perfect garden pelted with rain.
Under the unpruned branches
of a lemon tree Anatole beheld
the bright faces of pansies,
violas, violets, and knew he was
in heaven. "This garden," the seer
whispered in stumbling verses
on a Saint's Day in Liguria,
"was meant to be the whole world's
garden." I paid him in euros,
the currency of choice, and humming
old show tunes he danced off
into the dusk as the little street fair
broke up. All that night I heard
an angry sea rising against the shore
below my balcony and the winds
raiding the pines and knew morning
would break on a different world.
You ask how I, a man of no faith,
could believe in Anatole, could
take as fact this vision delivered
on boozy breath from behind
a white cotton beard held on

by rubber bands around the ears?
Even after I'd seen the seer's act
with Beniamino, the terrier mix
in blue trousers he'd taught to eat
with fork and knife, and to dab
his muzzle on a napkin, I believed.
That night the winds died, a morning
arrived, just as he'd predicted,
new light leaked between the shutters,
a light like no other. The waves
piled up along the shore as veined
as native marble, and to the west
a long arm of land descended
from nowhere, joining sea and sky,
a new land. It was the seer's vision
become flesh, it was Anatole—
or so we would learn to call it—
come back to earth as earth itself.

ALBION

On narrow roads twisting
between the farms, if farms
these were and not fallow
fields set off by stone walls
too low to keep anything
in or out. I'd been told
that when the west wind raged
local spirits—all the ghosts
of the unmourned—gathered
on the hilltops where no one
dared to go. We parked
in a little meadow shaded
by ancient birch and sycamore
going silver and gray under
the noon sun. Hand in hand
we climbed until the under-
growth separated us and she—
more nimble than I—took
the lead, and I followed until
the trees thinned out. The only
sound besides our breathing
was the silence. Beyond the first
clearing a stone wall stumbled
up and over a steeper rise.
Once there we saw the land
itself became confused as to
where to go. What, I thought,
could possibly be waiting
beyond still another grove
of birch and sycamore?
That was forty years ago
or more. We were still
young or young enough,
and new to the adventure,

so of course we kept going,
not in the hope of finding
Celtic arrowheads or human
skulls purified by time
and weather, or bronze relics
of lives we knew nothing of,
or what was actually there:
the exhausted chalky soil
of this depleted island
my father fought for. High
above, the clouds moved
against a pure blue sky
or perhaps it was the sky
that moved and everything
else stopped, like the two
of us, listening. Listening
for what? I ask myself now.
Call and response from bird
to bird or the sough of wind
stuttering through the trees,
the voices of a forgotten past?
I can't recall how long we
stood there nailed to the spot,
hand in hand, expectant,
as though anything
could tell us where we were.

THE GATEKEEPER'S CHIILDREN

This is the house of the very rich.
You can tell because it's taken all
The colors and left only the spaces
Between colors where the absence
Of rage and hunger survives. If you could
Get close you could touch the embers
Of red, the tiny beaks of yellow,
That jab back, the sacred blue that mimics
The color of heaven. Behind the house
The children digging in the flower beds
Have been out there since dawn waiting
To be called in for hot chocolate or tea
Or the remnants of meals. No one can see
Them, even though children are meant
To be seen, and these are good kids
Who go on working in silence.
They're called the gatekeeper's children,
Though there is no gate nor—of course—
Any gatekeeper, but if there were
These would be his, the seven of them,
Heads bowed, knifing the earth. Is that rain,
Snow, or what smearing their vision?
Remember, in the beginning they agreed
To accept a sky that answered nothing,
They agreed to lower their eyes, to accept
The gifts the hard ground hoarded.
Even though they were only children
They agreed to draw no more breath
Than fire requires and yet never to burn.

NIGHTSHIP

"Ceuta," I said. "I would like to go to Ceuta." "Go?" said the little ticket seller inside his cage, "you think the ship will go?" I asked if there was a saving on a round-trip ticket. He looked at the clock, which seemed to have stalled at a quarter to three & laughed, "You plan on returning?" He pushed an elaborate document across the counter & told me to sign my life away. On the dock I watched them loading small trucks with their Berber drivers into the hold as the oily waters off the pier began to turn from blue to black. It had been a brilliant, cloudless day. Beside the road to Algeciras I'd suddenly seen the Atlas Mountains emerging from their haze and thought, Africa, a whole new world! Once we were away a golden sun hovered off the straights for a long minute & then inched into the sea. I could hear water crashing into the hull & beneath that the steady beating of the engine & beneath that the wind whispering "Ceuta" in my good ear. At last my heart began to slow. Starless, the sky gave away nothing.

IN ANOTHER COUNTRY

A man spreads out dried fruit
on an old blanket and lets the flies
descend in a frenzy. When I try to shoo
them away he squats down to eye level,
takes my right hand delicately in his,
shakes his head, and mumbles
what might be a prayer or words
of advice or a curse. I don't know
because no one here—neither the sellers
nor the buyers—speaks a language
I understand. An old grandfather
whose white hair halos his head
sits cross-legged on the damp grass
smoking his pipe, his eyes closed.
His wares: a pyramid of stained teeth.
Shall I assume he is the dentist
of the town? There is no town, only
fields of long grass blowing in the wind
and beyond the wind the gray mountains.
A young woman, her forehead
and cheeks a web of delicate tattoos,
holds out a bowl of red powder.
Her eyes are so alive I have to
look away. She licks a forefinger,
then jabs it into the powder, and offers
me a taste. Blue and white pennants
fly from the tent poles. Women and children
on muleback stream down from the hills
or from nowhere. The powder tastes
like nothing I know, not bitter like
orange rind nor sweet like ground
rose petals nor bland like dyed flour.
I had heard there were storks nesting
on the haystacks and on the tallest

chimneys of the remote villages
and that wild, black-winged falcons
circled the fields all day keeping
watch over the land, feeding on whatever
came to rest. I saw none of that;
the only birds were tiny and caged,
beating their wings against the bars,
chattering like distant voices in dreams.
I've forgotten how I got there. I know
I knelt to a cold stream to wash my face
and wakened to music, an odd beat,
a melody I'd heard before. I followed
the sound over a rise to the open field
where the sun poured down its grace
on the long grass, the animals, the men
and women. The wind kept prodding
at my back as though determined
to push me away from where I was,
fearful, perhaps, I would come to rest.

BY THE WATERS OF THE LLOBREGAT

Two women and a small girl—
perhaps three or four years old—resting
in the shade of the fir trees.

From far off the roar of the world
coming back one more time.
First a few words tossed back

and forth between awakening men
and then the machines
talking to themselves in the language

they share with the heavenly bodies—
planets, dust motes, distant solar systems—
that know what needs to be

done and do it. So long ago,
you think, those days, so unlike these,
blessed by favorable winds

and forgotten in the anthems
we hummed on the long walk home
from work or the childish fables

we tried to believe. No one notices
the small girl and her caretakers
are gone and no one huddles

in the shade of the fir trees.
The air, brilliant and calm, stays
to witness, the single cloud lost

between heaven and here stays,
the mountains look down and keep
their distance, somewhere far off

the sea goes on working for itself.
By the waters of the Llobregat
no one sits down to weep for the children

of the world, by the Ebro, the Tagus,
the Guadalquivir, by the waters
of the world no one sits down and weeps.

III

A DOZEN DAWN SONGS, PLUS ONE

First the windows gray, then
go black again, but gray is
on the way. Williams lights up
and says, "It's on the way," but
I can't hear him over the over-
head cranes. I don't look up
because up is not sunlight
breaking above the eastern
hills or even rain clouds
meant to cool our fevers or
telephone wires clogged with
bad news. Up is the flat steel
ceiling from midnight till now.

—◦—

8 a.m. and we punch out
and leave the place to our betters,
the day-shift jokers who think
they're in for fun. It's still Monday
2,000 miles and fifty years
later and at my back I always
hear Chevy Gear & Axle
grinding the night-shift workers
into antiquity.

—◦—

A warm breeze from
nowhere and even the rats scent
the first perfumes of what's
to come, waken, and slide
invisibly into the upper air
to contest the world. Surrender

nothing and never, their motto,
if they have one. They must be
unionized.

◄o►

        The river works.
No one flips a switch, no one
shouts "Ready! Set! Go!" no one
writes a memo, it just runs
at its own sweet will its whole
blue-brown length toward five burned
lakes and seven seas.

◄o►

        We wait,
the night-shift owls, puffing out
our spent breath into the pure air
of 1951. A weak sun not
worth fighting for rises
behind the great brick stacks
of the brewery. War is
everywhere but we don't go because
the streetcar won't come.

◄o►

        If I had
a Milky Way I'd share it
with the sparrows picking
about the piss-speckled
snow, if I were reliable and hardy
and had wings I'd pick
about the piss-speckled snow
with the sparrows.

—◁o▷—

        Ragged
flights swarm the upper branches
of the elms only to abandon
their roosts and wheel
across the sky they've wiped
clean, back and forth, back
and forth they wipe until
no clouds or divine signs are left.
Must be some tremor only they
can feel or hawk stink or hint
of human treachery.

—◁o▷—

        Three mock
oranges do not an orchard make
but will do for now. Light blows
in from Ontario every
which way, hot and cold,
until the owner of the vacant lot
(who also owns the orchard)
kicks off the covers and calls for
sleep and dreams of her, the one
he'll never know.

—◁o▷—

        Half of us are
women. Think of that! Women,
women alone rising from
single beds meant for sleeping,
women in pairs, women with men
yearning to be free of us,
the men they met last night

or last century. "Give me
liberty or give me liberty,"
their anthem, and they mean it.

◄o►

                              One two
three four seconds and Harvey
yells again for Mona to get
her fat ass up. Don't she
know it's Monday workday.
The weekend—the last one, *the
one*—is long gone and Harvey's
got to have his coffee and his
oatmeal and his lunch box packed
just right, right now.

◄o►

                         One two three
four the scuffed black boots down
the stairs. "Does the bitch ever get
anything right?" Slam goes
the outside door, while upstairs
the teakettle sirens its answer . . .
Then quiet, the actual quiet
of public lives in private places.
6:30 a.m., the city of dreams.

◄o►

There was music. Not
the trite tunes of the blind stars
circling unseen or the gnashed jazz
the trolleys carved
into the avenues or the bad-assed
anthems of the airwaves—

of John Lee, Baby Boy
and Big Maceo——, not even
the music of the immortals,
Bird, Diz, Pres, music of bone
and breast, and breath, music
never heard before. Or again.

—◄◦►—

                                West
through Toledo, on past Flat Rock
going north. The sign is gone. Leo's
prewar '39 Chevy four-door
doing its dance routine: a little slide,
a little hold, a little slide on
black ice the devil delivered along
with two bald tires and two good
retreads. The sign's gone, the one
that said "Heaven Ahead" (or was it
Wyandotte?). Sunup behind us,
last night dissolving in the brine
of light. Coming home one
last time, yes we are!

—◄◦►—

                                Oh
to be young and strong and dumb
again in Michigan!

URBAN MYTHS

Slow learner though I am, it took me one night
to discover that rain in New York City
is just like rain in Detroit. It gets you wet.

Even in the Village the streets empty out
long before midnight. The comedy clubs
stay open, but no one comes out or goes in.

If there's music, it's the music in your head,
the same music that became the theme song
to every late night walk under the moon.

In Detroit no one walks under the moon
much less talks to it or to the unseen stars
that years ago we stopped believing were there.

As for midnight walks in the rain, in Detroit
they're regarded as urban myths like dance halls,
night baseball, or Fourth of July weekends.

From Brooklyn, across the East River
from New York, you can actually see
the parades, the picnics, and the fireworks.

The lovers crowd the Brooklyn promenade
waiting for hours for the final darkness to fall,
full of hope that at last Manhattan will ignite.

But it never does. It's exactly like Detroit,
with more people, more money, and two rivers
instead of one and often a hint of an ocean.

Brooklyn is different, the auto plants hum
night and day. Most of the workers are old
and look even older in their full beards,

prayer shawls, and black bib overalls.
They're glad to make union wages, they feel
useful punching in and out. When they're too old

to work they cross the Williamsburg Bridge
to the city on warm evenings to stroll
under a canopy of stars and the same moon

that left Detroit before I finished high school.
The more spiritual ones bike the Brooklyn Bridge
to Manhattan in hope of having a vision.

They come back with amazing souvenirs,
illustrated Apocrypha, tiny reproductions
of Ms. Liberty, and rumors of a savior

who rose from Michigan in 1928,
rumors I helped create with my tales
of the magic dogs who saved the synagogues.

Everything I've written here is true,
and the cities—Brooklyn and Detroit—
are actual, and people still live in them,

people you might love were you to venture
east, like the Magi on their mad quest
to touch a star and pass into history.

I still go back each year to Detroit
to relive my long childhood in the houses
that burned down ages ago, to walk alone

the streets paved with gold and to get wet.

RAIN IN WINTER

Outside the window drops caught
on the branches of the quince, the sky
distant and quiet, a few patches of light
breaking through. The day is fresh, barely
begun yet feeling used. Soon the phone
will ring for someone, and no one
will pick it up, and the ringing will go on
until the icebox answers with a groan.

The lost dog who sleeps on a bed of rags
behind the garage won't appear
to beg for anything. Nothing will explain
where the birds have gone, why a wind rages
through the ash trees, why the world
goes on accepting more and more rain.

THE ANGEL BERNARD

A gray row of corrugated huts
hunkering down in rain.
Across the way the fire burns
night and day though unseen
in sunlight. Bernard wakens
to the aroma of warming milk
and burned coffee. Later we'll say
he had the bearing of an angel
with clear eyes, a wide brow,
thick golden curls. His mother,
home from the night shift,
prepares his day, so he rises
to stand on the cold linoleum.
Ford Rouge, where she works,
goes on burning and banging,
but neither notices. It's their life.
Nonsense, you say, how can the life
of an angel include a Ford plant
where new life is tortured
into things? You saw the girl Mary
in a rose gown shyly bowing
before a dazzling Gabriel, his pale
wings furled, this in an empty
church in Genoa, the painting stained
but the scene unforgettable: That
was an angel bathed in his own light,
bearing the gift of a God, a presence
from another world. When Bernard
bows to dip bread in his coffee
his mother lays one hand down
on his bare nape as though she knows
he will die eleven years from now
in a fiery crash on US 24 on his way
to Dayton and thus leave his sons

behind. In this world the actual
occurs. In November the rain
streams skyward in cold sheets,
the fires burn unseen, the houses
bear down, separate and scared.

GODSPELL

I

About life I can say nothing. Instead,
half-blind, I wander the woods while
a west wind picks up in the trees
clustered above. The pines make
a music like no other, rising and
falling like a distant surf at night
that calms the darkness before
first light. How weightless
words are when nothing will do.

II

There was a season of snails, cankers, green slugs,
gophers I never saw, and then a short autumn
without a harvest, and the brown vines I tried
to burn with that year's leaves. A lifetime passes
in the blink of an eye. You look back and think,
That was heaven, so of course it had to end.

III

The gray dove on my windowsill
is still moaning over yesterday's
smashed eggs. But now the first
jackhammer breaks down
the dawn with its canticle
of progress. The garbage truck,
the street sweeper take their turns.
And the birds of the air and the beasts
of the field? They take their lumps
today and everyday, saith the TV.

FROGGY FRENCHMAN

No, not in the flesh—if Jesus was ever
in ordinary flesh—but in the faces
of the Christian ladies, heads held high
chanting their sorrows and joys for all
to share. He had turned away, Froggy said,
from sacred things since he was old enough
to pay his way. And here he was half-gone
on muscatel when he felt the soul soar
loose from the wreck of his body, all
350 misshapen pounds of it. No, not
in church, but on "the damn crosstown
streetcar running late."
                              A distant
Sunday night in the City of Dreams,
Froggy on his way to his weekend
of the usual low notes, cheap cigars,
Michigan wine, and stud poker, when Jesus
"come a knockin'." At Twelfth Street
the trolley stopped and a dozen ladies
mounted, each in her best flowered dress,
each with her worn Bible in hand,
each one blessed and glowing. "Changed
my life," Froggy says—for maybe
the hundredth time—though how
is hard to say.
                    Orphan of destiny,
descendant of voyagers, fur traders,
whiskey priests run amok in the final
wilderness, Froggy takes his ease on
the battered throne of history—a sprung
barrel chair—his tiny slippered feet
resting on a mismatched ottoman
out on the driveway. Sunday's
his day, he tells us. Sleeps late,

breakfasts on OJ and sips of "Morgan
Davis"—a consecrated beverage—,
and delivers his great truths to anyone
slow enough or dumb enough to listen.

LOUIE LIES

Louie lives by lying. He must always lie
all day long, and thus he craves fellowship.
He lies about the sunrise: "It was golden,
a great ball of fire clearing the rooftops,
sending the mockingbirds into wild screeches
as they scurried deeper into the branches
of the Atlas cedar." Actually the day
began slowly as the winter overcast
burned off above the treetops. The phone rings.
It's Louie. He's found a huge diamond ring
buried in his sock drawer. He has no idea
how it got there. "When I turn it toward
the light it gives off blue and yellow rays
like nothing ever seen. Would you like it?"
He'll be over within the hour. I make coffee,
turn on the classical music station
to hear Bach's Chaconne for the hundredth time.
When the bell rings it's Louie with a copy
of *The Watchtower*, his forehead beaded
with sweat, his eyes huge, his jeans sagging
under the weight of his new belly. Nothing
is said about the ring. Instead he tells me
about the women he met on his way over.
"One was from Prague, raven-haired,
pale as a ghost, six feet tall, right out of Poe.
The other spoke English, had been brought up
to believe she was Hemingway's daughter.
She chain-smoked Chesterfields. Both found God
in the Brooklyn Yellow Pages under
'Perishable Items.'" "Awake!" they'd cried
in chorus. Here he'd thought he was awake.
"Maybe I'll convert," he says, swirling his coffee.
He's tried Orthodox Judaism, Zen,
psychoanalysis, downhill racing,

organic farming, LSD. He shakes his head,
his wild black curls flashing in the noon light,
refuses more coffee, and rises to leave.
He has a lesson with his Latin teacher,
a young refugee from the Vatican
who wants to bear his child. The door closes
behind him, and the final notes of the Bach
scrape over and over. The record is stuck,
the DJ with the fake Irish accent is out
to lunch or drunk. I open *The New York Times.*

ZERO FOR CONDUCT

The bartender says, "Please," and then suggests
they go somewhere else to finish their fight.
He's had it. Night after night, the story
always the same: Zero just wants a place

in which to quietly ruin his life—
the words are his—and Estelle just requires
he live in a torment of her design.
1948, Miami Beach, Zero

farther down on his luck than even I,
waiting tables in the last Jewish diner
in Christendom, peeling potatoes, learning
fry cooking from an ex-con from Fresno.

So the four of us—I had a sidekick
in Cuban porno films teaching me Spanish—
set out for the Topper where Zero worked
until the night he lay down on the parquet,

face down, and begged Jesus Christ to kill him.
The audience had hissed, so he pissed his pants.
Tonight in the warm moonlight the world seems
full of possibility. At the sky's edge the stars

open and close their eyes as though flirting
with our little band of four sure losers.
I can hear the ocean sighing out there
where the invisible enters my sight

to become a cliché. Zero suddenly stops,
stamps out his cigarette, points heavenward
to announce that the one God of his boyhood
is hiding his face behind the light show

and won't appear this side of death
unless it's the sea out there churning at rest.
Then he dubs Estelle Queen of the Night:
"Ascend to your throne!" He tries to lift her

by the elbows, but the weight of her prattle,
constant and incomprehensible, holds
her earthward. Why I woke the next morning
just after the false dawn on someone's couch

to hear Zero at prayer, wrapping *tfilim,*
I'll never know, nor what silenced Estelle
at last, nor why the cold sea swallowed the sky
nor why I've chosen you to tell this to.

THE GIFT OF WINTER

Today the alder outside my window
motionless, the forsythia
holding its breath, the last smear

of fog burnt away so the morning
can enter the long memory
of winter, clear and uncorrupted.

Twelve years old, I tramped the back alleys
searching for something I couldn't
name or describe and found cinders

jeweled with tiny points of light
that could cut; I found handwritten,
scented letters, gifts from the future,

their words frozen in the weather—
"Paola, there's never a right time,"
written in a straight, manly hand that collapsed

from exhaustion. There were trees there too,
a row of tattered Chinese elms
to shade the past year's garbage,

a fenced-in copper beech thicker
than a sedan, its leafless
branches stiffening in wind.

There was always that wind, unnamed,
defiant, whistling in the face
of winter and not this odd calm

risen from nowhere outside
my window and closing in. Back then
when the year's worst blizzards

whited out the old neighborhood,
there was always new life aching
to break through and held back

by nothing I could do to stop it.

A HOME AWAY

The dawn is slow in coming. Instead light
leaks from the streetlamps, the few parked cars
take shape, here a house, there a tree's in sight.

The upholsterer from Shangri-La sleeps in.
Saturday settles on the city of man
as it seldom does (the odds are six to one).

He dreams of home, the fabled city
he returns to only in darkness, for only
in darkness is he a boy again, agile and happy.

If he had a wife her name would be Hilda,
if he had a son, the son would be seven or younger,
for like him he would never grow older

so far from home, so far from the life
he was meant for, the life waiting patiently
in that far-off city with Hilda for wife.

On tiptoe she enters his room without a sound
to strangle the silence as a wife should.
If the clock watches it says not a word.

Everything is silent, the houses drop their eyes,
cars hold their breath, the trees freeze,
a man dreams, and no birds sing as they please.

POSTCARDS

I

Blank headstones that mirror
the mourners and the kids
sweating in hand-me-down suits.
Someone must have thought
these rituals keep the dead down
at least until the trumpets blow
and the fire-breathing angels
come to harrow our houses.

II

A wild spring in the fields
of the foothills smeared with lupine
and poppy. The great peaks, cold,
white, breathless, looked down
with disdain. Three finches,
then a fourth, black-capped,
darted in and out of the light,
reminding us it was not too late.

III

No one bent down to pick up
the cotton work-glove stained
with pollen, the sad remains
of campfires, ashes, glass, stiff
crusts of bread, unread letters.
It was all there silently
telling us what was waiting.

IV

Off in the distance you can hear
a hammering and then the quick
explosions of the jackhammer
carving the hardpan. Where there
was space there will be rooms
without windows, rectangular,
severe, there will be high shelves
sagging under the weight of seashells,
feathers, sallow photographs,
blank journals, wedding rings.

TURKEYS

What is this thing if it's
not language? But to one
great dead poet it was

"a nuance of sound
delicately operating
upon a cataract of sense."

A few lines later good Doc
Williams calls his own remark
stupid and states flat-out

a nuance can't operate
on anything. It's "all in
the sound," he writes. Or maybe

it's not, maybe it's nowhere. Just
then a knock on my door:
my Brooklyn neighbor,

Jean-Claude, requires
instruction in our prosaic tongue
and the ways of his oven——

new, electronic, and baffling.
He's roasting a turkey
with bacon and thyme——

the French way, the way
his mother did back
in '56, when he got

home from "Indochine."
That word plops
down between us, deprived

of both music and charm,
though back in '39
I thrilled to hear my boy-

hood suddenly dubbed
an "historic era" as the Bakelite
little Admiral incanted

the sudden magic of "Stuka,"
"blitzkrieg," "panzer,"
"Me 109," "Maginot,"

"collaborator." The next year
spring came late if
at all. In early May I

heard water rushing
in the alleys and knew some-
one or something would

send us summer. Later summer
came, hot and sullen,
one defeat at a time, joylessly

over the rooftops of
heaven. But for now Jean-
Claude and I pore over

the impenetrable argot
of the maker's manual searching
for a nuance of sense

so the brand-new oven
avec temporisateur
can operate on the sixteen-

pound puckered tom,
stuffed and trussed for
the event, though no more

trussed and stuffed than we,
should evening ever come.

HOW TO GET THERE

Turn left off Henry onto Middagh Street
    to see our famous firehouse, home
        of Engine 205 and

Hook & Ladder 118 and home also to
    the mythic painting "Fire under
        the Bridge" decorating

the corrugated sliding door. The painting
    depicts a giant American flag
        wrinkled by wind

and dwarfing the famous Brooklyn Bridge
    as it stretches as best it can
        to get a purchase

on Manhattan. In the distance a few dismal
    towers and beyond the towers
        still another river.

A little deal table holds a tiny American
    flag—like the one Foreman held
        as he bowed to

receive gold at the '68 Olympics in Mexico
    City—; this actual flag is rooted in
        a can of hothouse

roses going brown at the edges and beginning
    to shed. There's a metal collection
        box bearing the

names of those lost during the recent burnings.
   Should you stop to shake the box—
      which is none

of your business—you'll hear only a whisper.
   Perhaps the donations are all
      hush money,

ones, fives, tens, twenties, or more likely
   there are IOUs and the heart
      of Brooklyn

has gone cold from so much asking.
   Down the block and across
      the street, a man

sleeps on the sidewalk, an ordinary
   man, somehow utterly spent,
      he sleeps through

all the usual sounds of a Brooklyn noon.
   Beside him a dog, a terrier,
      its muzzle resting

on crossed paws, its brown eyes wide
   and intelligent. Between man
      and dog sits

a take-out coffee cup meant to receive,
   next to it a picture of Jesus—
      actually

a digital, color photograph of the Lord
   in his prime, robed and
      though bearded

impossibly young and athletic, and—
as always—alone. "Give
what you can,"

says a hand-lettered cardboard sign
to all who pass. If you stand
there long enough

without giving or receiving the shabby,
little terrier will close his eyes.
If you stand

there long enough the air will thicken
with dusk and dust and exhaust
and finally with

a starless dark. The day will become something
it's never been before, something for
which I have no name.

THE LAST SHIFT

I had been on my way to work as usual
when the traffic stalled a quarter mile
from the railroad crossing on Grand Blvd.
Then I saw the moon rise above
the packing sheds of the old Packard plant.
The moon at 7:30 in the morning.
And the radio went on playing
the same violins and voices I didn't
listen to each morning. Back in the alley
the guys in greasy, dark wool jackets
were keeping warm by a little fire
made from fence posts and garage doors
and tossing their empty wine bottles
into the street where they shattered
on the frosted roofs of cars and scattered
like chunks of ice. A police car dozed
across the street, its motor running.
I could see the two of them eating
sugar doughnuts as delicately as two
elderly women and drinking their coffee
from little Styrofoam cups. Soon the kids
would descend from these lightless houses,
gloved and scarved, on their way to school
with tin boxes of sandwiches and cookies.
They would slide on the ice and steal
each other's foolish hats and laugh
while they still could, their breath
pushing out into the morning air
in little trumpets of steam. I wondered
if anyone would step from the faceless
two-storied house beside me, all of its
rooms torn into view, its connections
and tubing gone, the furniture gone,
the floors ripped up for firewood.

Up ahead I could hear that the train
had stopped, the bells went on ringing
for a minute, the blinking arms of light
went from red to nothing. Around me
the engines began to die, and then
my own went. It was strangely quiet,
another town or maybe another world.
I could feel a deep cold slowly climbing
my legs, which wouldn't move, my eyes
began to itch and blink on a darkness
I had never seen before. I knew
these tiny glazed pictures—a car hood,
my own speedometer, the steering wheel,
the windshield fogging over—were the last
I'd ever see. These places where I had lived
all the days of my life were giving up
their hold on me and not a moment too soon.

ACKNOWLEDGMENTS

Special thanks to Ann Close, Philip Levine's dedicated friend and editor at Knopf. Thanks also to Deborah Landau, the director of the Creative Writing Program at NYU, where Levine completed his long career teaching poetry. I owe a special debt to the gifted young poet Elisa Gonzalez, who worked with me on every aspect of this book. It is more fully realized because of her. My greatest thanks is to Franny Levine, Phil's inspiration and bedrock, who entrusted us with this book.

Thanks to the editors of the following publications in which these poems appeared:

Blackbird: "The Privilege of Power"

The Cortland Review: "Assembly," "The Gift of Winter" (as "Distant February"), "The Privilege of Power"

Field: "A Wall in Naples and Nothing More"

Five Points: "History," "Nightship," "Tall Tales," "The Absent Gardener," "The Privilege of Power"

The Forward: "Zero for Conduct"

Fugue Literary Journal: "Anatole," "The Gift of Winter"

Harper's Magazine: "A Dozen Dawn Songs, Plus One"

Kestrel: "Immortal Birds"

The New Yorker: "1934," "By the Waters of the Llobregat," "In Another Country," "I Was Married on the Fiftieth Birthday of Pablo Neruda," "More Than You Gave," "Pennsylvania Pastoral," "The Future," "Turkeys"

MacGuffin: "A Wall in Naples and Nothing More"

Michigan Quarterly Review: "The Last Shift"

Ploughshares: "The Angel Bernard"; parts of "A Dozen Dawn Songs" and "Godspell" were published under the title "Postcards."

Poetry: "How to Get There," "Inheritance," "My Brother, the Artist, at Seven," "Froggy Frenchman," "The Gatekeeper's Children"

The Southern Review: "A Home Away," "Your Turn"

The Threepenny Review: "Albion," "Leaves," "Louie Lies," "Urban Myths"

Tungsten Press: "Godspell"

The Village Voice: "Office Hours"

Philip Levine was born in 1928 in Detroit. He was formally educated in the public schools and at Wayne University (now Wayne State University). After a succession of industrial jobs in Detroit, he left the city for good, first attending the writing workshop at the University of Iowa, where he received an MFA in 1957. He then lived in various parts of the country before settling in Fresno, California, where he taught at the state university until his retirement. He also taught in many other places, including Columbia; Princeton; Brown; the University of California, Berkeley; and New York University, where he served as poet in residence for over a decade.

He received many awards for his books of poems, including two National Book Awards—in 1980 for *Ashes: Poems Old and New* and in 1991 for *What Work Is*—and the Pulitzer Prize in 1995 for *The Simple Truth*. He also won the Ruth Lilly Prize in Poetry and the Wallace Stevens Award. In 2006 he was elected a chancellor of the Academy of American Poets, and in 2011 was appointed poet laureate of the United States.

After he retired from teaching at California State University, Fresno, in 1992, he divided his time between Fresno, California, and Brooklyn, New York. He died in 2015.

A NOTE ON THE TYPE

The text of this book was set in Centaur, the only typeface designed by Bruce Rogers (1870–1957), the well-known American book designer. A celebrated penman, Rogers based his design on the roman face cut by Nicolas Jenson in 1470 for his Eusebius. Jenson's roman surpassed all of its forerunners and even today, in modern recuttings, remains one of the most popular and attractive of all typefaces.

The italic used to accompany Centaur is Arrighi, designed by another American, Frederic Warde, and based on the chancery face used by Lodovico degli Arrighi in 1524.

TYPESET BY NORTH MARKET STREET GRAPHICS, LANCASTER, PENNSYLVANIA
PRINTED AND BOUND BY BERRYVILLE GRAPHICS, BERRYVILLE, VIRGINIA
DESIGNED BY IRIS WEINSTEIN